How Is a Bandage Like a Worm?
Medicine Imitating Nature

Walt Brody

Lerner Publications • Minneapolis

Lerner Publications Company
A division of Lerner Publishing Group, Inc.
241 First Avenue North
Minneapolis, MN 55401 USA

For reading levels and more information, look up this title at www.lernerbooks.com.

Main body text set in Billy Infant Regular. Typeface provided by SparkType.

Editor: Brianna Kaiser **Photo Editor:** Sarah Kallemeyn
Lerner team: Sue Marquis

Library of Congress Cataloging-in-Publication Data

Names: Brody, Walt, 1978- author.
Title: How is a bandage like a worm? : medicine imitating nature / Walt Brody.
Description: Minneapolis, MN : Lerner Publications, [2022] | Series: Lightning bolt
    books—imitating nature | Includes bibliographical references and index. | Audience:
    Ages 6-9 | Audience: Grades 2-3 | Summary: "Medical practices are forever evolving
    with technological advancements. But where does inspiration for new ideas come
    from? This title explores how biomimicry is used in surgeries, in healing wounds,
    and more" —Provided by publisher.
Identifiers: LCCN 2020012422 (print) | LCCN 2020012423 (ebook) | ISBN 9781728404189
    (library binding) | ISBN 9781728418407 (ebook)
Subjects: LCSH: Biomimicry—Juvenile literature. | Medical technology—Juvenile literature.
    | Inventions—Juvenile literature. | Nature—Juvenile literature. | Medical innovations—
    Juvenile literature.
Classification: LCC R855.4 .B76 2022 (print) | LCC R855.4 (ebook) | DDC 610.28—dc23

LC record available at https://lccn.loc.gov/2020012422
LC ebook record available at https://lccn.loc.gov/2020012423

Manufactured in the United States of America
1-48476-48990-11/12/2020

Table of Contents

Inventions from Nature

Doctors are smart. They treat sick people. Some doctors invent new technology to help people.

Doctors sometimes get technology ideas from nature. This is called biomimicry. *Bio* means "living." *Mimic* means "to copy."

Doctors use many types of equipment, including microscopes, to study bacteria and other living things.

5

A Worm's Glue

Sandcastle worms live in the ocean off the coast of California. They are small, but they are great builders.

Sandcastle worms make a glue that is strong and works on wet surfaces.

Sandcastle worms produce a special glue. This glue works underwater. They use the glue to build reefs.

Scientists are researching the worms at a university in California. They are interested in the worms' glue because it's strong and works on wet surfaces. This makes it very useful.

Scientists at UC Santa Barbara study sandcastle worms' glue because it's really strong.

Some scientists believe sandcastle worms' glue could be used as a bandage on a fetus's sac.

Some scientists think the glue can help fetuses. They think the glue can protect the fetus's sac from breaking. That's how a bandage is like a worm.

A Spider's Web

Many people are afraid of spiders, but spiders are very helpful. They eat lots of bugs. And they have a really cool home, a spider's web!

Spiders use silk to make webs. They produce strong silk in their spinnerets. They spin it into beautiful patterns.

All spiders produce silk, but different types of spiders produce different types of silk.

Doctors are interested in using spider silk to make thread for stitches.

Doctors want to use spider silk for medical purposes. The silk fibers can be braided together to make a very strong thread.

Doctors are interested in using the threads for stitches. Stitches hold wounds closed until they are healed.

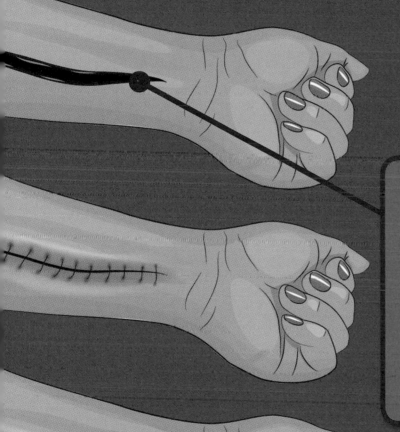

If a person has a deep cut (*top arm*), stitches can be applied (*middle arm*) that hold the cut closed until it heals (*bottom arm*).

A Sticky Burr

Velcro was invented in the 1950s. It is used on shoes, backpacks, and many other things.

Velcro tape

Burrs have little hooks that make it stick to clothing and animal fur.

George de Mestral was a Swiss inventor. He went on hikes with his dog. He noticed that burrs would stick to his clothing and to his dog's fur.

Some plants have burrs.
They are the plant's seeds.
They have little hooks that
stick to an animal's fur. Then
the burr will drop somewhere
and sprout.

Burrs stick to animal fur so they can spread to other areas and sprout new plants.

Velcro has little hooks on it just as a burr has.

De Mestral made Velcro with little hooks like on a burr. This invention is used on medical supplies. It is used for knee braces, breathing masks, and much more.

A Shark's Skin

Sharks are one of the most feared ocean creatures. We can learn from them too. Their skin might help us fight germs.

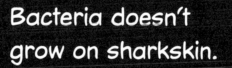

Bacteria doesn't grow on sharkskin.

Sharkskin is made of very small scales. Bacteria cannot grow on them. Scientists have invented a way to print sharkskin onto surfaces.

Some types of bacteria keep people healthy, while other types can make people sick.

Bacteria can make people sick. This invention can help stop the spread of bacteria. That will make humans healthier.

The Future of Medicine

Some doctors are trying to use bananas to fight cancer. Cancer makes people very sick. Doctors found that banana peels can help map and find skin cancer in people. They are trying to make a device to find cancer cells. The device would kill the cancer with electricity. This might cure people with skin cancer.

Glossary

bacteria: tiny living things that can cause disease

biomimicry: getting ideas for inventions from nature

fetus: a stage of a baby's growth before it is born

invention: a device or process that is made to help people

reef: a ridge of rock, sand, or coral on the ocean floor

spinneret: the part of a spider's body that produces silk

sprout: when a plant starts to grow from a seed

stitches: threads that hold wounds closed so they can heal

Learn More

Kiddle: Bionics Facts for Kids
https://kids.kiddle.co/Bionics

Kiddle: Medicine Facts for Kids
https://kids.kiddle.co/Medicine

Montgomery, Sy. *The Great White Shark Scientist.* New York: Houghton Mifflin Harcourt, 2021.

The School Run: Spiders
https://www.theschoolrun.com/homework-help/spiders

Swanson, Jennifer. *Beastly Bionics: Rad Robots, Brilliant Biomimicry, and Incredible Inventions Inspired by Nature.* Washington, DC: National Geographic, 2020.

Waxman, Laura Hamilton. *Doctor Tools.* Minneapolis: Lerner Publications, 2020.

Index

Photo Acknowledgments

Image credits: Monkey Business Images/Shutterstock.com, p. 4; kurhan/Shutterstock.com, p. 5; © Fred Hayes for the University of Utah, p. 6; © Thewellman at Wikimedia Commons, p. 7; Ryosuke Yagi/flickr (CC BY 2.0), p. 8; adike/Shutterstock.com, p. 9; Ian Fletcher/Shutterstock.com, p. 10; Nicky J Graham/Shutterstock.com, p. 11; a17/Shutterstock.com, p. 12; Artemida-psy/Shutterstock.com, p. 13; Ekaterina43/Shutterstock.com, p. 14; Suzanne Tucker/Shutterstock.com, p. 15; A Daily Odyssey/Shutterstock.com, p. 16; JPC-PROD/Shutterstock.com, p. 17; Shane Myers Photography/Shutterstock.com, p. 18; aspas/Shutterstock.com, p. 19; Leigh Prather/Shutterstock.com, p. 20.

Cover images: Blue Planet Archive/Alamy Stock Photo; Anton Starikov/Shutterstock.com.